Two Dramatizations

I. Dido—the Phœnecian Queen
II. The Fall of Troy

Virgil

(Contributor: J. Raleigh Nelson)

(Translator: Frank Justus Miller)

Alpha Editions

This edition published in 2024

ISBN : 9789362514844

Design and Setting By
Alpha Editions
www.alphaedis.com
Email - info@alphaedis.com

As per information held with us this book is in Public Domain.
This book is a reproduction of an important historical work. Alpha Editions uses the best technology to reproduce historical work in the same manner it was first published to preserve its original nature. Any marks or number seen are left intentionally to preserve its true form.

PREFACE

The epic is a drama on gigantic scale; its acts are years or centuries; its actors, heroes; its stage, the world of life; its events, those mighty cycles of activity that leave their deep impress on human history. Homer's epics reënact the stirring scenes of the ten years' siege of Troy, and the perilous, long wanderings of Ulysses before he reached his home; Vergil's epic action embraces the fall of Troy and the never-ending struggles of Æneas and his band of exiles till Troy should rise again in the western world; Tasso pictures the heroic war of Godfrey and his crusaders, who strove to free the holy city of Jerusalem; and Milton, ignoring all bounds of time and space, fills his triple stage of heaven, earth, and hell with angels, men, and devils, all working out the most stupendous problems of human destiny.

Such gigantic dramas could be presented on no human stage. But in them all are lesser actions of marked dramatic possibility. Notable among these are the events culminating in the death of Hector, the home coming of Ulysses and his destruction of the suitors, Satan's rebellion and expulsion from heaven, and the temptation and fall of man. All these furnish abundant material for the tragic stage; but all leave much to be supplied of speech and action before the full-rounded drama could take form. In the Æneid alone is found, among the minor parts which make up the epic whole, a dramatic action well-nigh complete—the love story of Æneas and Dido.

The ordinary student of Vergil is too much engrossed with an intensive study of the text, and has too near a view of the poem, to appreciate how fully this story is worked out in detail; how its speech, action, and events all lead to a dramatic climax. There is need only here and there of an interpolated lyric upon some suggested theme, a bit of Vergil's description of action or feeling expressed in the actor's words, an interjected line to relieve the strain of too long speech—all else is Vergil's own, ready to be lifted out of its larger epic setting and portrayed upon the stage.

In arranging and translating this epic tragedy, the authors have made only such minor additions and alterations of the original as seemed necessary from the dramatic point of view. Prominent among these are the introduction of lyrics at certain points, the obviously necessary curtailing of the banquet scene by the omission of the long narrative of Æneas, and the removal behind the scenes of the final tragedy of Dido's suicide. The lyrical parts have been set to original music in sympathy with the themes; stage action and scenery are suggested by outline drawings of the different settings; and idealized figures and costumes are reproduced from ancient vases and bas-reliefs. These figures have, in some cases, been assigned by scholars to other subjects; but they may be taken, for the purposes of the present work, as illustrative of the characters designated.

With full consciousness of the shortcomings of the work, but with the hope also of assisting the student in school and home to a fuller appreciation of the power and beauty of Vergil, this volume is respectfully presented to the public.

PREFACE TO THE SECOND EDITION

The first edition of this volume, containing only the Dido: An Epic Tragedy, a dramatization of the love story of Æneas and Dido, was published in 1900, and met with a gratifying success. Teachers of Vergil have found the book an interesting supplement to their study and presentation of the text; and in numerous instances high-school and college classes have staged the play with most excellent results.

The book has been out of print for several years; but the continued demand from teachers who desire to use it has made a second edition desirable. This is accordingly offered in the present volume, under a new title, and containing a second dramatization from Vergil—this from the second Æneid, the story of the Fall of Troy.

F. J. M.

CHICAGO, 1908

I
Dido—The Phœnician Queen

THE ARGUMENT

For ten years the Greeks had besieged Troy, and on the tenth they took and utterly destroyed that ancient city. The inhabitants who had escaped captivity and the sword, wandered in exile to many quarters of the earth. Now the chief band of exiles was led by Æneas, son of Venus and Anchises, and son-in-law of Priam, king of Troy.

After many adventures on land and sea, Æneas came, in the sixth year, to Sicily, where he was kindly entertained by Acestes, king of that land, and where his aged father died and was buried. Thence setting sail in the summer of the seventh year, he approached the shores of Africa. Here a violent storm arose which scattered and all but destroyed the Trojan ships. Æneas, with a number of his companions, was cast upon a desert coast, where they passed the night in gloomy forebodings. In the early morning, Æneas and Achates set forth to explore the land, and came to the newly founded city of Carthage.

Now Phœnician Dido, also, with a band of exiles, had fled from her native Tyre, to escape the persecutions of her brother, Pygmalion, who had already slain Sychæus, her husband. And to the land of Africa had she come, and built her a city, even the city of Carthage.

And so these two, Æneas, prince of Troy, and Dido, fugitive from Tyre, now meet in distant Africa and live the tragedy which fate has held in store.

THE PERSONS OF THE DRAMA

ÆNEAS, prince of Troy, and leader of the Trojan exiles.

ACHATES, confidential friend of Æneas.

ILIONEUS, a Trojan noble.

DIDO, the queen of Carthage.

ANNA, sister of Dido.

BARCE, nurse of Dido.

IOPAS, a Carthaginian minstrel.

IARBAS, a Moorish prince, suitor for the hand of Dido.

JUNO, queen of Jupiter and protectress of the Carthaginians, hostile to Troy.

VENUS, the goddess of love, mother of Æneas, and protectress of the Trojans.

CUPID, son of Venus, god of love.

MERCURY, the messenger of Jupiter.

Maidens, Courtiers, Soldiers, Attendants, Servants, etc., in Dido's train.

Nobles, Sailors, etc., in the band of Æneas.

THE PRELUDE

[For music, see p. 57]

Arma virumque cano, Troiæ qui primus ab oris

Italiam, fato profugus, Lavinaque venit

Litora, multum ille et terris iactatus et alto

Vi superum, sævæ memorem Iunonis ob iram,

Multa quoque et bello passus, dum conderet urbem,

Inferretque deos Latio: genus unde Latinum

Albanique patres atque altæ mœnia Romæ.

Musa, mihi causas memora, quo numine læso,

Quidve dolens, regina deum tot volvere casus

Insignem pietate virum, tot adire labores

Impulerit. Tantæne animis cælestibus iræ?

ACT I

Dido—The Phœnician Queen

ACT I. SCENE 1

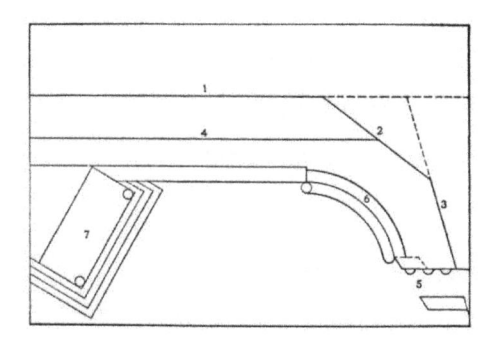

Early morning; the open square before the temple of Juno on a height near Carthage. In the distance (see cut, 1, 2, 3) appear mountains, and at their foot lies the city, clustered about the harbor where ships are riding at anchor. The effect of elevation is increased by the unfinished columns and the tree-tops just showing above the low marble wall which encloses the square. This scene (4) is set nearer than 1, 2, 3, to increase the perspective.

At the first wing on the right (5), a colonnade, leading to a flight of steps, forms the entrance from the city below. On the same side, along the wall, is a broad marble seat (6), shaded by a wild crab tree, pink with bloom. The dark rug on the step before it is strewn with fallen petals. On the left is the front of the temple (7). Two large columns of white marble flank three broad steps leading to the platform. Above these columns, the architrave bears a frieze representing scenes from the Trojan war. Before the temple door is an altar on which fire is burning.

At the rise of the curtain, a chorus of Carthaginian maidens, clad in white, are seen kneeling before the altar on the temple steps; they sing a greeting to the dawn.

Hymn to the Dawn

[For music, see p. 61]

Wake, Aurora, Wake!

Come, rosy-fingered goddess of the dawn,

The saffron couch of old Tithonus scorning;

Fling wide the golden portals of the morning,

And bid the gloomy mists of night be gone.

Hail, Aurora, Hail!

The dewy stars have sped their silent flight,

The fuller glories of thy rays expecting;

With rosy beauty from afar reflecting,

Thy Orient steeds come panting into sight.

Rise, Apollo, Rise!

Send forth thy healing rays to greet the world,

Upon the lands thy blessed radiance streaming;

Arise, and fling afar, in splendor gleaming,

The banners of thy golden light unfurled.

Enter Æneas and Achates, on their way into the city, evidently attracted hither by the singing. Æneas is resplendent in full armor. Achates wears the Phrygian costume: long trousers of brown, a tunic of deep old blue, ornate with embroidered patterns in gold and purple thread; over this a traveling cloak of brown. He carries two spears. The maidens withdraw and as their voices grow fainter Æneas and Achates kneel before the altar. The light brightens. A bugle call in the distance rouses them from their devotion. They arise. Enter Venus, dressed as a huntress.

Venus (Æneid, I. 321-324):

I crave your grace, good sirs. If my attendant maids

Have chanced to wander hither, quiver-girt, and clad

In tawny robes of fur, the trophies of the chase,

Or with triumphant shouts close pressing in pursuit

The foaming boar,—I fain would know their course.

Æneas (326-334):

Fair maid,

No huntress of thy train have we beheld, nor heard

The clamor of their chase.—But oh, no mortal maid

Art thou! Th' immortal beauty of thy face and voice

Proclaim thee goddess. Art thou Phœbus' sister then?

Or some fair nymph? Whoe'er thou art, we crave thy grace:

Be merciful and tell beneath what sky at length,

Upon what shores we 're tossed. For ignorant of men

And land we wander, driven on by wind and wave

In vast conspiracy.

Full many a victim slain

Upon thine altars shall repay thine aid.

Venus (335-350):

For me,

I claim no homage due the gods. Behold a maid

Of ancient Tyre, with quiver girt and feet high shod

With purple buskin—such our country's garb. Thou seest

Before thee Punic realms; the city and its men

Are both alike Phœnician; but around them lie

The borders of the Libyans, hardy race, unmatched

In war. The city owns the sway of Dido, late

Escaped from Tyre and from her brother's threat'nings. Long

The story of her wrongs, and devious its way;

But here I'll trace the outline of her history.

Her husband was Sychæus, of his countrymen

The richest far in wide possessions; well beloved

By his ill-fated bride was he, whose virgin hand

In wedlock's primal rite her sire had given him.

But Tyre's domain Pygmalion her brother held,

Surpassing all in crime. Between these Tyrian lords

A deadly feud arose. With impious hand and blind

With love of gold, Pygmalion, at the altar-side,

With stealthy, unsuspected stroke Sychæus slew;

And little recked he of his sister's doting love.

Æneas (III. 56, 57):

O awful, quenchless thirst of gold! 'T was ever thus

That thou hast spurred the hearts of men to deeds of blood.

Venus (I. 351-370):

He long concealed the deed with wanton, feigned excuse,

And mocked his sister, sick at heart, with empty hopes.

In vain: for in the visions of the night the shade,

The pallid shade of her unburied husband came;
The cruel altar and his piercèd breast he showed,
And all the hidden guilt of that proud house revealed.
He bade her speed her flight and leave her fatherland,
And showed, to aid her cause, deep buried in the earth,
An ancient treasure, store of silver and of gold
Uncounted.
Thus forewarned the queen prepared her flight
And bade her comrades join her enterprise. They came,
Whom hatred or consuming terror of the prince
Inspired. A fleet of ships at anchor chanced to lie
In waiting. These they seized and quickly filled with gold;
Pygmalion's treasure, heaped with greedy care, was reft
Away upon the sea, a woman leading all.
They reached at last the place where now the mighty walls
And newly rising citadel of Carthage stand.
But who and whence are ye? and whither do ye fare?

Æneas (372-385):

O goddess, if beginning at the first the tale
Of direful woes on land and deep I should relate,
The day, before my story's end, would sink to rest.
From Troy (perchance the name of Troy has reached your ears)
Borne over many seas, the fitful tempest's will
Has brought us to these shores.
Æneas am I called,
The Pious, for that in my ships I ever bear
My country's gods, snatched from our burning Troy. My fame
O'erleaps the stars. My quest is Italy, a land
And race that mighty Jove hath promised me. For this,

With score of vessels staunch I braved the Phrygian sea,

By Venus' star directed and by fate impelled.

But oh, alas for Venus' star, alas for fate!

Scarce seven shattered barks survive the waves, and I—

And I, a beggared stranger, wander helpless here,

A fugitive from all the world.

Venus (387-401):

Whoe'er thou art,

Full sure am I the gods must love thee well, since thou

Through dangers manifold hast reached this Tyrian realm.

But haste thee and with heart of cheer seek out the queen.

For lo, thy friends are rescued and thy fleet restored,

Unless in vain my parents taught me augury.

For see, those joyous swans are fluttering to the earth,

Which, swooping from the sky, but now the bird of Jove

Was harrying. As they, with fluttering wings and cries

Of joy regain the earth, so, by this token know,

Thy ships and comrades even now are safe in port,

Or with full sails the harbor's mouth are entering.

Then fare thee on, and follow where the path of fate

May lead.

As Venus vanishes from the temple steps she is illumined in rosy light.
Æneas (402-409):

Achates, see the bright refulgent glow

Upon her face! 'T is light divine! And from her locks

Ambrosial, heavenly odors breathe! Her garments sweep

In stately folds, and she doth walk, a goddess all,

With tread majestic!

Lo, 't is Venus' self! O stay,

My heavenly mother, stay! Why dost thou, cruel too,

So often mock thy son with borrowed semblances?

Why may we not join hands, each in his proper self,

And speak the words of truth? Ah me! She's vanished quite,

And I am left forlorn!—

Deeply moved, he follows her vanishing figure.

Achates, seeking to divert Æneas, leads him to the parapet and points out to him the life awakening in the city below (422-429).

Behold this city with its gates and mighty walls,

And well-paved streets, where even now the Tyrians

With eager zeal press on their various toil. See there,

Some build the citadel and heave up massive stones

With straining hands; while some a humbler task essay,

And trace the furrow round their future homes. Behold,

Within the harbor others toil, and here thou seest

The deep foundations of the theater, where soon

Shall rise huge columns, stately set, to deck the scene.

Æneas(430-437):

Yea all, like busy bees throughout the flowery mead,

Are all astir with eager toil. O blessed toil!

O happy ye, whose walls already rise! But I,—

When shall I see my city and my city's walls?

He remains in deep dejection.

Achates, observing the pediment of the temple itself (456-458):

But here, O friend, behold, in carvèd imagery,

Our Trojan battles one by one, that mighty strife

Whose fame has filled the world. Here see Achilles fierce,

The sons of Atreus,—and, alas, our fallen king!

Æneas, deeply affected (459-463):

What place, Achates, what far corner of the world
Is not o'erburdened with our woes? O fallen King,
E'en here our glorious struggle wins its meed of praise,
And those our mortal hopes defeated and o'erthrown,
Are mourned by human tears.
Therefore our present cares
Let us dismiss. This fame shall bring us safety too.

Achates, continuing to examine the pediment (467, 468):

See how the Greeks are fleeing, pressed by Trojan youth!
While here, alas, our warriors flee Achilles' might.

Æneas (469-478):

And here behold the ill-starred Rhesus' white-winged tents,
Where fierce Tydides slays his sleeping foe; and drives
Those snowy steeds to join the Grecian camp, before
They graze in Trojan meadows or the Xanthus drink.
Alas poor Troilus, I see thee too, ill-matched
With great Achilles. Prone thou liest within thy car,
While in the dust thy comely locks and valiant spear
Are basely trailed.

Achates (479-482):

Here to Minerva's temple come
Our Trojan dames with suppliant mien and votive gifts;
With locks dishevelled, self-inflicted blows, and tears;
But all for naught. All unappeased the goddess stands
With stern averted face, nor will she heed their prayers.

Æneas (483-487):

Thrice round the walls of Troy the fell Achilles drags

The body of my friend.—O Hector, Hector! Here

He sells thy lifeless body for accursed gold,

While aged Priam stretches forth his helpless hands.

Achates (488-497):

And here behold thyself amid the Grecian chiefs

In combat raging. See the swarthy Memnon's arms,

And that fierce maid, who, clad in gleaming armor, dares

To lead her Amazons and mingle in the fray.

Music is heard in the distance, flutes and zithers leading a chorus.

But hark! The distant strains of music greet my ear,

As of some stately progress fitly timed with flute

And zither.

See, it is the queen, who with her band

Of chosen youths and maidens hither takes her way.

Æneas (498-501):

How like Diana when she leads her bands by swift

Eurotas, or on Cynthus green, while round her press

A thousand graceful creatures of the wood; but she,

With shoulder quiver-girt, a very goddess moves

With stately tread among the lesser beings of

Her train. To such an one I liken yonder queen.

They conceal themselves in the foreground behind the columns of the temple. Dido, accompanied by her bands of courtiers, crosses the stage and ascends the temple steps. She seats herself on the throne which has been placed for her at the temple door.

Dido throughout this act is dressed in white, the symbol of her widowhood. Her dress, worn without himation, is of light filmy stuff draped in the Greek style, and unornamented save for a border of gold thread. Anna wears a dress of delicate blue, elaborately embroidered about the edges with a Greek pattern in gold thread. Her himation, wrapped gracefully about her, is a tender shade of rose pink.

In Dido's train all classes are represented, gayly dressed courtiers, soldiers, and peasants. The men wear cloaks of dark blue and of rich brown over their tunics. The women are clad in dresses of cream color, pink, and faint green.

When all are on the stage, the general effect should be a mingling of pink, blue, brown, green, and white, which harmonize with the tints of the marble, of the flowering crab tree, the blue sky, and the purple mountains.

Suddenly Ilioneus and his following of Trojans appear. They wear the Phrygian costume, but over it the long brown traveling cloak. The singing ceases, the guards lower their spears, and great excitement reigns.

Æneas, aside (509, 510):

Achates, can it be? What! Antheus, and our brave

Cloanthus and Sergestus too?

Achates, aside (511-514):

Yea, all our friends

Whose ships the raging storm hath parted from our fleet

And driven far away. O joy! Come, let us go

And grasp their hands in greeting.

Æneas, aside (515-521):

Nay, not so, for still

Our fortune in the balance hangs. Here let us see

What fate befalls our friends, where they have left their fleet,

And why they hither come. For chosen messengers

In suppliant aspect do they seek this sacred fane,

While round them rage the mob.—But see, Ilioneus speaks.

Dido has arisen and with a gesture bids the soldiers stand aside. She sends a page to lead Ilioneus to her throne. Ilioneus kneels before her; she extends the scepter, which he touches.

Ilioneus, rising and standing before the queen (522-558):

O Queen to whom the king of heav'n hath given to found

A city and to curb proud nations with the reins

Of law, we Trojans in our need, the sport of winds

On every sea, implore thee, spare a pious race

And look, we pray, with nearer view upon our cause.

We have not come to devastate with fire and sword

The Libyan homes, or fill our ships with plundered stores.

Such violence and such high-handed deeds a race

By fate o'ercome may not attempt. There is a place,

Hesperia the Greeks have named it, ancient, rich

In heroes, and of fertile soil. Œnotrians

Once held the land; but now, as rumor goes, their sons

In honor of their mighty leader have the place

Italia called. To this our seaward course was bent:

When suddenly, upstarting from the deep, all charged

With tempests, did Orion on the shallows drive

Our vessels, with the aid of boisterous winds and waves,

Through boiling, overtopping floods and trackless reefs,

And put us utterly to rout. To these thy shores

A few of us have drifted. But alas! what race

Of men is this? What land permits such savage deeds

As these? We are refused the barren refuge of

The sandy shore; they seek a cause for mortal strife,

And will not that we set our feet upon the land.

What though the human race and mortal arms are naught

To thee; be sure that gods regard the evil and

The good. We had a king, Æneas, more than peer
Of all in justice, piety, and warrior's might.
If by decree of fate he still survives, if still
He draws the vital air of heav'n, and lies not low
Amid the gloomy shades, fear not, and let it not
Repent thee that in deeds of mercy thou didst strive
To be the first. We still possess both towns and lands
Upon Sicilia's isle; Acestes too, renowned,
And born of Trojan blood, is ours. Our only prayer,
That we may draw our shattered fleet upon the shore,
And in the forest shade renew our weakened beams
And broken oars. That thus, if to Italia's realms,
Our comrades and our king regained, 't is ours again
To hold our way, with joy we may that selfsame land
And Latium's borders seek. But if in vain our hope,
And if, loved father of the Teucri, thou art held
By Libya's billows and no more we may upon
Iulus rest our hopes, then let us seek the land
And homes reserved for us, whence, setting sail, we came
To these thy hostile shores, and make Acestes king.

Shouts of applause from the Trojans.
Dido, with modest bearing (562-578):

Let not a fear disturb your souls, O Teucrians;
Away with all your cares. My cruel fortune and
My yet unstable throne compel me thus to guard
My bounds with wide and jealous watch. Who knows not well
Æneas and his race, their city Troy, their brave,
Heroic deeds? Who has not seen the far-off flames
Of their great war? We carry not such brutish hearts

Within our breasts, nor yet does Phœbus yoke his steeds

So far from this our land. Seek you the mighty west,

The land of Saturn's reign, or where your foster-king,

Acestes, rules within Sicilia's borders? Lo,

In safety will I send you forth and gird you with

My aid. Or would you share with me this realm? Behold,

The city which I build is yours. Draw up your ships.

To Trojan and to Tyrian will I favor show

In equal measure. Would that your Æneas' self,

Conducted by the same o'er-mastering gale, were here!

My messengers along the shore will I despatch,

And bid them search the farthest bounds of Libya,

If he in wood or city, rescued from the waves,

May chance to stray.

She despatches courtiers to seek Æneas. Æneas and Achates, meantime, are greatly agitated by her words.

Achates, to Æneas, aside (582-585):

Æneas, what thy purpose now?

Thou seest all is well. Thy fleet and captains all,

Save one, are rescued. One we saw ourselves o'erwhelmed

Within the deep. All else thy mother's prophecy

Upholds.

At this, Æneas suddenly reveals himself, to the great surprise of both Trojans and Carthaginians.

Æneas, to Dido (595-609):

O Queen, before thee, whom thou wouldst behold, am I,

Æneas, Prince of Troy, late rescued from the waves

Of Libya. O thou, who only o'er the woes,

The dreadful woes of Troy hast wept, who to thy town

And home dost welcome us, the leavings of the Greeks,

Who every peril of the land and sea have faced,

And lost our all: we may not thank thee worthily,

O Queen, nor yet the Trojan race, what remnant still

In distant lands in exile wanders. May the gods

A fitting gift bestow upon thee; if indeed

They feel a true regard for pious souls, if e'er

The truth and conscious virtue aught avail. But thee—

What blessed age, what mighty parents gave thee birth?

Whate'er my fate, while to the sea the rivers flow,

While o'er the mountains' rounded sides the shadows drift,

While on the plains of heav'n the stars shall feed, so long

Thine honor and thy name and praises shall abide.

The queen is silent with amazement, while Æneas greets his friends amid general rejoicing.

Dido, recovering from her astonishment (615-630):

What fate, thou son of heav'n, decrees these perils vast?

And what the power that drives thee on our savage shores?

And art thou that Æneas whom to Ilium's prince,

Anchises, on the bank of Phrygian Simois,

The kindly Venus bore? And now do I recall

That Teucer once to Sidon came as suppliant;

For exiled from his native Salamis he came.

'T was at the time when fertile Cyprus bowed beneath

My father's might, and by the victor's sway was held.

From that time on, thy name, and all the Grecian kings,

And the fortunes of thy city have been known to me.

Nay, Teucer's self, though foeman, sang the praise of Troy,

And said that he himself from ancient Trojan stock

Had sprung.

Wherefore, O princes, come and make my halls

Your own. An equal fate has willed that I, like you,

The sport of many toils, should find a resting place

Within this land. With grief acquainted, I have learned

To comfort hapless wanderers oppressed with grief.

They prepare to leave the scene. Dido despatches men to bear gifts to the Trojan fleet, and proclaims a banquet for the ensuing night in honor of Æneas and the Trojan princes.

Æneas, to Achates (643-655):

Go, speed thee, friend, to where, upon the sandy beach,

Our comrades camp about the ships. This joyful news

To young Ascanius bear, and bid him come with thee

To Dido's town.

Exit Achates.

To other Trojans:

Go ye, and fetch from out the ships

The treasures that we saved from Ilium's fall: the robe,

Stiff wrought with golden pattern, and the flowing veil

All interwov'n with bright acanthus' yellow bloom,

Those beauteous robes of price which Argive Helen brought

From rich Mycenæ when to Pergama she came,

Her mother's wondrous gift. And bring the scepter fair

Which once Ilione, the eldest daughter of

Our monarch, bore; the pearl-set necklace, and the crown,

Its double golden circlet spangled o'er with gems.

The Trojans withdraw to do his bidding. The music sounds, and as the entire court moves from the scene, Dido sends some of her maidens back to throw incense upon the flames. They kneel upon the steps and Anna advances to the altar. As the smoke ascends, Dido and Æneas turn to follow the rest. Curtain.

ACT I. SCENE 2

A place in the deep, green forest. Ferns and flowers strew the ground and the sunlight falls through the branches in flecks of gold. In the foreground are two great moss-grown rocks, on one of which sits Cupid, draped with garlands of wild flowers, shooting his arrows at a heart-shaped target hung from the branches of a tree in the center of the stage. At one side sits Venus, absorbed in deep, troubled meditation. She has resumed the flowing draperies befitting a goddess. Pink or canary yellow will harmonize with the scene.

Venus (657-662):

Ah me! I fear this Tyrian hospitality;

For well I know their faithless hearts and lying tongues.

And ever, mid the anxious watches of the night,

The savage threats of Juno agitate my soul.

If only this fair queen might feel the pulse of love

For this my hero son, then would her purposes

Of amity be fixed, and my anxiety

Be set at rest.—But how accomplish my design?

Suddenly her face is lighted with a new thought. She goes to Cupid and addresses him with insinuating gentleness.

Venus, to Cupid (664-688):

O son, my comrade and my only source of might,

O thou, who scorn'st the giant-slaying darts of Jove,

To thee I come and humbly pray thy fav'ring aid.

How on the sea, from land to land, thy brother fares,

Pursued by Juno's unrelenting hate, is known

To thee, and often hast thou mingled in my grief.

Now Tyrian Dido holds him, and with fawning words

Delays his course; and much do I distrust and fear

The shelter which our envious rival Juno gives.
For, in this pregnant crisis of affairs, be sure
She will be active. Wherefore now my mind is bent
With wiles to take the queen, ere Juno steel her heart,
And hold her fast in passion's net; that at the hest
Of Juno she her present purpose may not change,
But by a mighty love for this her Trojan guest
She may be bound to work my will.
Now hear thy part:
Obedient to the summons of his doting sire,
The youthful prince Ascanius goes to Dido's town
With gifts which Ocean and the flames of Troy have spared;
Him, lapped in sleep, will I to far Cythera bear,
Or hide him in my sacred fane on Ida's top,
Lest he should know what we intend, and thwart our plans.
Do thou, if only for a night, assume the form
Of young Ascanius, that, when the queen with joy
To her embrace shall take thee, when amid the wine
And feasting she shall hold thee in her arms and kiss
Thy lips, thou mayst inflame her unsuspecting heart
With the subtle fires of love.

As she unfolds her plan, Cupid is filled with delight. He struts up and down, comically imitating Ascanius. When his mother has finished, he hastens to pick up his scattered arrows, puts them in his quiver, and struts off, looking back for his mother's smile of approval. Curtain.

ACT I. SCENE 3

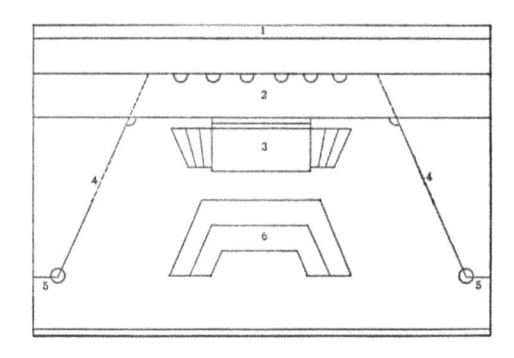

A banquet hall in Dido's palace. Across the back of the stage is a colonnade (2), raised above the level of the hall. Through the columns there is a view (1) out over the moonlit sea. Two broad steps lead from the colonnade to a landing, from which again three steps at each side descend to the level of the hall (3). At the second wing (4) on each side, curtained doorways open into the side rooms, from which the servants hurry with viands for the table. At the first wing (5), half columns form the corner of the wall. In the center a sort of triclinium (6) is set for the feast, a broad, three-sided table flanked by couches upholstered in Tyrian purple and having pillows of blue and gold.

When the curtain rises, the moonlight is streaming down through the columns upon the scene. A tripod burns before the triclinium. Otherwise there is no light except as it flashes from the side rooms when the curtains are parted for an instant. Servants are strewing the banquet table with flowers and bringing in dishes of gold.

The antique bronze lamps, hung between the columns, are lighted one by one, till the scene is brilliant with light and color.

Music is heard within. The servants hastily finish their work. The royal party enters along the colonnade. Dido is still clad in white, but Anna and the other ladies of the court have assumed himations of royal purple, royal blue, brilliant yellow, and deep green. Æneas has laid aside his helmet and greaves, but still wears his breastplate of mail, although he carries on his shoulder a cloak of royal purple.

The Carthaginians are more elaborately and richly dressed than in the first scene. The Trojans have put aside their outer cloaks, and wear tunics gayly embroidered in colors. The servants wear tunics of white.

The guests recline upon the couches. Æneas is in the seat of honor, while Dido has placed the supposed Ascanius upon the couch at her side. Many of the Carthaginians and the Trojans fill the hall.

Dido rises. There is silence through the room. She intones the invocation.

Dido (731-735):

[For music, see p. 69]

O Jove, thou lord of gods and men, since 't is from thee

The rites of hospitality proceed, ordain

That this may be a day of joy to us of Tyre

And these the Trojan exiles; let its fame go down

To our descendants. May the god of wine and joy,

And fost'ring Juno grace and celebrate the day.

The entire company repeats the invocation in unison. When they have finished, all bow and Dido pours forth the libation upon the table. Touching the cup to her lips, she passes it to the guests of honor.

While the cup is passing about, Iopas and his chorus sing.

Song of Iopas (suggested by 740-746)

[For music, see p. 72]

I

Of the orb of the wandering moon I sing,

As she wheels through the darkening skies;

Where the storm-brooding band of the Hyades swing,

And the circling Triones arise;

Of the sun's struggling ball

Which the shadows appall

Till the menacing darkness flies;

2

Of the all-potent forces that dwell in the air,

With its measureless reaches of blue;

The soft floating clouds of gossamer there,

And the loud-wailing storm-rack too;

Of the rain and the winds

And the lightning that blinds

When its swift-darting bolt flashes through;

3

Of the marvels deep hid in the bowels of earth,

In the dark caves of Ocean confined,

Where the rivers in slow-trickling rills have their birth,

And the dense tangled mazes unwind;

In the deep under-land,

In the dim wonderland,

Where broods the vast cosmical mind.

4

Of the manifold wonders of life I sing,

Its mysteries striving to scan,

In the rippling wave, on the fluttering wing,

In beast and all-dominant man.

'T is the indwelling soul

Of the god of the whole,

Since the dawn of creation began.

Dido, who has been gazing upon Æneas in rapt admiration (753-756):

Now come, my guest, and from the first recount the tale

Of Grecian treachery, thy friends' sad overthrow

And all thy toils; for lo, the seventh summer finds

Thee wand'ring still in every land, on every sea.

Æneas, rising (II. 3-13)

Thou wouldst that I should feel a woe unspeakable,

O Queen, and tell again how all our Trojan power

And kingdom, endless source of grief, the Greeks o'erthrew:

Those sad events which I myself beheld, and in

Whose fabric I was wrought a part. Who, though he be

Of fierce Achilles' band, or in the train of hard

Ulysses, telling such a tale could hold his tears?

Now night sinks down the steeps of heaven, while setting stars

And constellations summon us to rest. But if

So strong is thy desire to know the story of

Our woe, and hear Troy's final agonies rehearsed,

Though at the very thought my soul within me shrinks

And has recoiled in grief, I will begin the tale.

All the Trojans and Carthaginians crowd around the tables, seating themselves to listen. As all faces are turned toward Æneas, he sinks back upon his couch, overcome with emotion. There is a moment of silent sympathy. Curtain.

ACT II. SCENE 1

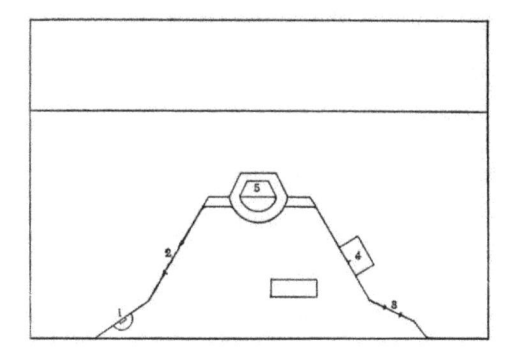

Dido's chamber. At the left, in front, is a shrine (1). An antique bust with an inscription above it, visible in the light from the glowing censer, indicates

that it is sacred to Synchæus. Two broad steps raise it slightly from the level of the stage. On the same side in the middle a door (2), flanked by half columns. At the right, first wing, a door (3); half-way back on the same side (4), a curtained recess in which are hung Dido's brilliant robes. In the center of the background (5), is a window overlooking the city and harbor, which show in the distance when the window is opened. It is reached by two steps covered with rugs, and the seats about the three sides of the recess are richly upholstered in green and gray.

Anna and Dido both wear simple white, while Barce, the aged nurse, is clad plainly in brown.

Barce lies asleep on a couch near the shrine, her face lighted by the glowing flame. Anna is asleep on a couch in the foreground.

Dido sits at the window in the moonlight, looking out into the night. She gets up and moves restlessly about the room. She kneels before the altar, replenishing the incense. She comes finally to her sister, and, wakening her, tells of her struggle against the new love.

Dido (IV. 9-29):

O sister, what dread visions of the night invade

My troubled soul! What of this stranger lodged within

Our halls, how noble in his mien, how brave in heart,

Of what puissant arms! From heav'n in truth his race

Must be derived, for fear betokens low-born souls.

Alas, how tempest-tossed of fate was he! How to

The dregs the bitter cup of war's reverses hath

He drained! If in my soul the purpose were not fixed

That not to any suitor would I yield myself

In wedlock, since the time when he who won my love

Was reft away, perchance I might have yielded now.

For sister, I confess it, since my husband's fate,

Since that sad day when by his blood my father's house

Was sprinkled, this of all men has my feelings moved.

Again I feel the force of passion's sway. But no!

May I be gulfed within earth's yawning depths; may Jove

Almighty hurl me with his thunders to the shades,

The pallid shades of Erebus and night profound,

Before, O constancy, I violate thy laws!

He took my heart who first engaged my maiden love.

Still may he keep his own, and in the silent tomb

Preserve my love inviolate.—

Anna (31-53):

O dearer to thy sister than the light of life,

Wilt thou consume thy youth in loneliness and grief,

And never know the sacred joys of motherhood,

The sweets of love? And dost thou think, that in the tomb

Thy husband's sleeping spirit recks of this? Let be,

That never yet have other suitors moved thy heart

Which long has scorned the lords of Libya and of Tyre;

Let prince Iarbas be rejected and the lords

Of Africa's heroic land: wilt still against

A pleasing love contend? And hast considered then

Whose are the powers upon the borders of thy realm?

Here are Gætulia's cities, matchless race in war;

Here wild Numidians hedge thee round, and Ocean's shoals;

While yonder lies the sandy desert parched and wild,

Where fierce Barcæans range. Why need I mention Tyre's

Dark-looming cloud of war, thy brother's threats? For me,

I think that through the favor of the gods and care

Of Juno hath Æneas drifted to our shores.

And to what glory shalt thou see thy city rise,

What strong far-reaching sway upreared on such a tie!

Assisted by the Trojan arms, our youthful state

Up to the very pinnacle of fame shall soar.

Then pray the favor of the gods, and give its due

To sacred hospitality. Lo, to thy hand

Is cause of dalliance, while still the blustering winds

Of winter sweep the sea, Orion's storms prevail,

Their fleet is shattered, and the frowning heavens lower.

Dido, during this speech, has gone to her husband's shrine. There is a mighty struggle in her soul between love and duty.

Barce, wakened from her sleep and seeing her mistress pale and anguish-stricken, throws herself before her. Dido finally yields and reaches her trembling hand to quench the censer. The old nurse clings to her in terrified appeal. Dido frees herself from her. She quenches the flame and draws the curtain before the shrine. Old Barce sits sobbing before the darkened altar.

Meanwhile the light has been changing into dawn and the sea and harbor begin to be visible through the open window. Dido crosses the chamber, and after a moment's struggle draws back the curtains from before the recess where hang the brilliant garments laid aside during her widowhood. She takes down a purple mantle, and standing before a mirror, girds it about her with a golden girdle.

The sound of a trumpet and the shouts of the sailors are heard in the distance. Anna goes to the window, and seeing Æneas and his men below on the shore, draws Dido to the window. Dido gazes for a minute and then, filled with her new passion, goes forth with her sister to meet Æneas. Curtain.

ACT II. SCENE 2

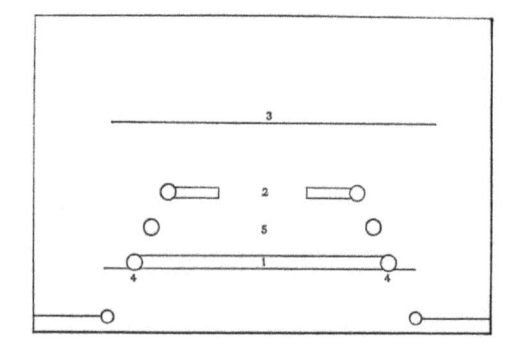

A fragrant nook on Mount Ida. Across the stage at the first wing a low, broad marble wall (1), forming one end of a colonnade which leads back to an arch (2), through which the distant sea is visible (3). The columns at the first wing (4) and the wall between them are over-clambered by a flowering vine, which has strewn its delicate yellow petals over the wall and the marble floor before it. Behind the wall (5) a garden of brilliant blossoms, with a path leading through it to the arch in the background. There is the pleasant sound of falling water.

Venus, seated upon the low marble wall is discovered keeping watch over Ascanius who lies asleep before her his pink body hidden in a drift of yellow petals. The deep blue himation, which has fallen in graceful folds across the wall behind her, forms a rich contrast in color to the delicate tints of the marble, of the flowers, and of her own dress of tender pink. Juno in a brilliant purple dress, approaching through the garden, comes upon her in a fury of wrath.

Juno (93-104):

Fair fame, in sooth, and booty rich thou shalt obtain,

Thou and thy boy, a lasting name, if by the guile

Of two divinities one woman is o'ercome!

Nor have I failed of late to see the jealous fear

In which thou holdest these our Carthaginian walls.

But come, in such a strife what motive can we have?

Nay, rather shall we not a lasting peace secure

By Hymen's bonds? Behold, thou hast what thou hast sought

With all thy soul: fair Dido burns with ardent love,

And feels its thrill of passion dominate her heart.

Then let us rule this people, thou and I, on terms

Of amity. Let Dido wed the Trojan prince,

And give to thee, as royal dowry, Tyria's lords.

Venus (107-114):

How mad th' opponent who would such fair terms refuse!

Or who would wish to strive by preference with thee!

If only fortune favor what thou hast proposed:

But of the fates am I uncertain, whether Jove

Be willing that the Trojan exiles and the men

Of Carthage reign in common and a lasting bond

Of amity cement. Thou art his wife. 'T is right

For thee by prayer to try his will. Do thou lead on,

I follow.

Juno (115-126):

Mine the task thou sayest. Now the way

In which the matter may be perfected in brief

Will I reveal. Do thou attend my words.—The queen,

Unhappy Dido, and Æneas, to the wood

Prepare to lead the hunt, when first to-morrow's sun

Hath reared his radiant head and with his shining beams

Revealed the world. On these, while beaters force the game,

And hem the glades with circling nets, will I a storm

Of rain and mingled hail pour down and rack the sky

From pole to pole. In all directions will they flee

Before the storm, and shield themselves in sheltering caves.

The queen and Trojan leader will together seek

The selfsame grot. And, if thy favoring purpose hold,

I shall in lasting union join and make them one.

Venus assents, and, bending over the sleeping boy, shows by a satiric smile that she perceives the purpose of her rival. Curtain.

Act II. Scene 3

A forest scene. Huge trees and moss-grown rocks. Across the back, a cliff in the face of which at the last wing on the left is the opening to a mighty cavern. Through the trees growing along the summit of this cliff, comes the shimmer of the distant sea.

Far and near through all the forest, trumpets are sounding. Attendants armed with spears and nets, and with hounds in leash for the chase, hurry across the scene. Dido, Anna, Æneas, Ascanius, followed by the entire court in brilliant array, cross the scene amid the flourish of trumpets.

All the costumes are very brilliant with gold, purple, deep blue, and wood green. Dido is dressed in purple and gold, Anna in brown and green with a leopard skin instead of a himation. Æneas is in full armor. All the Trojans and Carthaginians are dressed and armed for the chase.

One of the attendants has seated himself in the foreground to mend his broken bow. As the sound of the trumpets grows fainter, a band of Carthaginian youth, hurrying to join the hunt, descry him and stop to laugh at him, because he is left behind. He throws down his bow in disgust, and points in the direction of the hunt with a gesture of impatience.

Attendant (191-194):

Now look you, to our shores has come this Trojan prince

Whom Dido, our fair queen, has taken as her lord.

And now in dalliance fond the winter's days they spend,

Unmindful of their heaven-appointed destinies,

And taken in the subtle snare of base desire.

Approval on the part of all the youth.

Meanwhile it has grown darker, and there comes a crash of thunder. All flee in terror. As the storm increases, the courtiers flee across the scene in every direction. The trumpets are heard calling through all the woods.

At last, amid the crash of thunder and the roar of the tempest, Dido and Æneas enter, seeking a place of shelter. Discovering the cavern, they flee to that. Lightning flashes, the thunder roars, the wild cries of the nymphs are heard.

The scene closes in almost utter darkness. Curtain.

ACT III

ACT III. SCENE 1

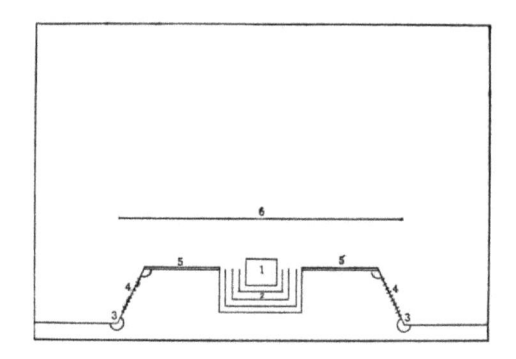

The temple of Jupiter Ammon in Libya. In the center of the stage an altar (1), raised high from the level of the stage by four broad steps (2). Pillars of barbaric form and decoration at the first and second wings (3), between which are hung curtains (4) of rich, oriental pattern. At the second wing a wall (5) joins the two pillars. In the distance (6), across a wide tract of desert, Carthage can be seen, showing only as a cluster of glimmering lights except when the lightning flashes fitfully along the horizon. The scene is lighted only by the glare of the altar fire.

Iarbas wears a robe of scarlet worked in gold.

Iarbas, kneeling before the altar, his face lifted defiantly upward (206-218):

O Jove omnipotent, to whom the Moorish race

From 'broidered couches pour their offering of wine,

Dost thou regard th' affairs of men? or is 't in vain

We tremble, father, when thou hurl'st thy thunderbolts?

And is it only aimless flashings that we fear,

And meaningless vain mutterings that fill the sky?

That vagrant queen to whom we gave within our bounds

A site whereon to build her town, a bit of shore

To till, and granted full possession of the place,

Hath this our suit disdained and to her realm received

Æneas as her lord. And now that puny prince,

That Paris, with his train of weaklings, and his locks

Perfumed, bedecked and sheltered by a Phrygian cap,

Hath carried off the prize.—And we, poor fools, bring gifts

Unto thy temple and adore an empty shrine!

Sullen mutterings of distant thunder. Curtain.

SCENES 2 AND 3

The temple colonnade, as in Act I. Scene 1. Æneas, surrounded by Achates, Ihoneus, and many other Trojans, is directing the work in the city below them. He has in his hands the plan of the citadel, which he is tracing for his countrymen. Mercury appears upon the temple steps, crosses the stage, and stands a moment behind Æneas and his companions, unnoticed.

Mercury, to Æneas, as the Trojans turn and discover him (265-276):

And can it be that thou art building here the walls

Of Tyrian Carthage, and uprearing her fair towers,

Thou dotard, of thy realm and thy great destiny

Forgetful! Jove himself, the ruler of the gods,

Who holds the heavens and earth and moves them at his will,

To thee from bright Olympus straight hath sent me here.

He bade me bear on speeding pinions these commands:

What dost thou here? or with what hopes dost thou delay

Upon the Libyan shores? If thou, indeed, art moved

By no regard for thine own glorious destiny,

Respect at least the budding hopes of him, thy son,

Who after thee shall hold the scepter; for to him

Are due the realms of Italy, the land of Rome.

While Mercury is giving his message, Dido, followed by her maidens, comes forth from the temple, and as she catches the import of his words, stands horror-stricken upon the temple steps, unnoticed by Æneas or his men, whose faces are turned intently toward Mercury.

Æneas, overwhelmed with astonishment, aside (281-294):

O Jove, and I had near forgot my destiny,
To oblivion lulled amid the sweets of this fair land!
But now my heart's sole longing is for Italy,
Which waits me by the promise of the fates. But how
From this benumbing passion shall I free myself?
How face the queen and put away her clinging love?

To his attendants:

Go ye, and swiftly call the Trojans to the shore;
Bid them equip the vessels quickly for the sea,
And frame for this our sudden voyage some fitting cause.

Mnestheus and the others withdraw to perform his commands. Æneas remains buried in deep thought. He turns and sees Dido standing before him. They gaze at each other in silence.

Dido (305-330):

And didst thou hope that thou couldst hide thy fell design,
O faithless, and in silence steal away from this
My land? Does not our love, and pledge of faith once given,
Nor thought of Dido, doomed to die a cruel death,
Detain thee? Can it be that under wintry skies
Thou wouldest launch thy fleet and urge thy onward way
Mid stormy blasts across the sea, O cruel one?
But what if not a stranger's land and unknown homes
Thou soughtest; what if Troy, thy city, still remained:
Still wouldst thou fare to Troy along the wave-tossed sea?
Is 't I thou fleest? By these tears and thy right hand—
Since in my depth of crushing woe I've nothing left—
And by our marriage bond and sacred union joined,

If ever aught of mercy I have earned of thee,
If I have ever giv'n thee one sweet drop of joy,
Have pity on my falling house, and change, I pray,
Thy cruel purpose if there still is room for prayer.
For thee the Libyan races hate me, and my lords
Of Tyre; for thee my latest scruple was o'ercome;
My fame, by which I was ascending to the stars,
My kingdom, fates,—all these have I giv'n up for thee.
And thou, for whom dost thou abandon me, O guest?—
Since from the name of husband this sole name remains.
What wait I more? Is 't till Pygmalion shall come,
And lay my walls in ruins, or the desert prince,
Iarbas, lead me captive home? O cruel fate!
If only ere thou fled'st some pledge had been conceived
Of thee, if round my halls some son of thine might sport,
To bear thy name and bring thine image back to me,
Then truly should I seem not utterly bereft.

Æneas, seemingly unmoved by her appeal (333-361):

I never shall gainsay, O Queen, that thy desert
Can equal all and more than all that thou canst claim;
And ever in the days to come 't will be my joy
Fair Dido to recall while memory serves me, while
My spirit animates these limbs.—To thine appeal
A brief reply. I did not hope to leave thy shores
By stealth—believe it or not—nor yet a husbands' name
Have I desired, nor have I claimed the marriage bonds.
If under omens of my own it were ordained
That I should live, and lay aside at will the weight
Of destiny, then first of all would I restore

My Trojan city and the dear remains of all
I called my own; old Priam's royal halls would still
Endure, and long ago would I have built again
Our ruined citadel of Pergama. But now
To mighty Italy Apollo's oracle,
To Italy his lots command that I repair.
This is my love and this must be my fatherland.
If thou, though born in distant Tyre, art linked to this
Thy Carthage in the land of Libya, why, I pray,
Shouldst thou begrudge to us, the Trojan wanderers,
Ausonia's land? 'T is fate that we as well as thou
Should seek a foreign home. My sire Anchises' shade
Invades my dreams with threats and admonition stern,
Whene'er with dewy shadows night o'erspreads the earth.
And when I think upon Ascanius and the wrong
That I am bringing on his head, though innocent,
My heart reproaches me that I am thwarting fate,
Which promised him the destined fields of Italy.
And now the very messenger of heav'n sent down
By Jove himself—I swear by both our lives—has brought
The mandate through the wind-swept air; I saw the god
Myself in open day invade thy city's walls,
And with these very ears I heard his warning voice.
Then cease to vex thyself and me with these complaints;
'T is not of mine own will I fare to Italy.

Æneas, as he speaks, has become as one seeing in vision the glorious future of his race. Dido, who has stood with averted face and scornful look, now turns upon him, in a passion of grief and rage.

Dido (365-387):

Thou art no son of Venus, nor was Dardanus
The ancient founder of thy race, thou faithless one:
But Caucasus with rough and flinty crags begot,
And fierce Hyrcanian tigers suckled thee. For why
Should I restrain my speech, or greater evil wait?
Did he one sympathetic sigh of sorrow heave?
Did he one tear let fall, o'er-mastered by my grief?
Now neither Juno, mighty queen, nor father Jove
Impartial sees; for faith is everywhere betrayed.
That shipwrecked beggar in my folly did I take
And cause to sit upon my throne; I saved his fleet,
His friends I rescued—Oh, the furies drive me mad!
Now 't is Apollo's dictate, now the Lycian lots,
And now "the very messenger of heaven sent down
By Jove himself" to bring this mandate through the air!
A fitting task is that for heaven's immortal lords!
Such cares as these disturb their everlasting calm!
I seek not to detain nor answer thee; sail on
To Italy, seek fated realms beyond the seas.
For me, if pious prayers can aught avail, I pray
That thou amid the wrecking reefs mayst drain the cup
Of retribution to the dregs and vainly call
Upon the name of Dido. Distant though I be,
With fury's torch will I pursue thee, and when death
Shall free my spirit, will I haunt thee everywhere.
O thou shalt meet thy punishment, perfidious one:
My soul shall know, for such glad news would penetrate
The lowest depths of hell.—

She works herself up to a frenzy, and as she finishes she turns to leave him with queenly scorn, staggers, and falls. Her servants carry her from the scene, leaving Æneas in agony of soul, struggling between love and duty. Curtain.

Act IV

ACT IV. SCENE 1

Dido's chamber as in Act II. Scene 1. Anna sits in the foreground, spinning. The old nurse, Barce, is bustling about, hanging up her mistress' brilliant robes, which she has cast aside for her old mourning gown of simple white. Dido is seated at the latticed window watching the Trojans in the harbor below prepare for their departure. She is weeping.

Barce, coming cautiously to Anna so that Dido may not hear (416-418):

Behold, how eagerly the Trojans launch their ships.

In their mad zeal they hurry timbers from the woods,

Unhewn and rough, from which to shape their masts and oars,

While from the city shoreward rush the fleeing men.

The shouts of the sailors are heard. Dido groans. Anna, hastily putting aside her work, goes to her sister, whose face is buried in her hands. Barce takes up the spinning, stopping at times to wipe her eyes.

Dido, lifting her face to her sister (416-418):

Thou seest, Anna, how they haste from every side,

And how the bustle of departure fills the shore.

The vessels float, the swelling sails salute the breeze,

And now the sailors crown the sterns with festive wreaths!

She gives way to her tears.

Anna, caressing her sister:

Alas, my sister, for thy sighs and grieving tears,

Thy love abandoned and thy trusting faith betrayed!

Dido (419-434):

If this great grief in expectation I have borne,

Then truly shall I patience have to bear it still.

But, sister, grant me in my woe this one request—

For yonder faithless one was wont to cherish thee

Alone, and trust to thee his heart; and thou alone

Dost know the fav'ring time and method of approach

To try the man:—go, sister, and in suppliant strain

Address our haughty foe: I took no oath with Greece

At wind-swept Aulis to o'erthrow the Trojan State,

Nor did I send a hostile fleet to Pergama,

Nor desecrate the sacred ashes of his sire,

That now he should refuse to bend his ear to me.

Go, say his hapless lover makes this last request:

That he wait an easy voyage and a fav'ring gale.

No longer do I ask a husband's love denied,

Nor yet that he abandon his fair land and realm;

Time, only time, I ask, a little space of rest

From this mad grief, till Fortune give me fortitude,

And teach me how to bear my woe.

Anna, preparing to go (412):

O love betrayed,

To what despair dost thou not drive the hearts of men?

Exit Anna.

Dido, at the window, watches her sister as she takes her way down to the harbor. When she can no longer see her in the gathering twilight, she turns with a sigh to her chamber.

The old nurse, Barce, totters to her. Dido places her head wearily on the old woman's shoulder. Barce, drawing her to a couch, tries to soothe her. Dido starts up in terror, as if she saw some fearful shape. She flees before it to her husband's shrine, and is only recalled from the fancy when she finds the curtains drawn before it.

Barce comes tremblingly to her. Dido in bitter remorse draws the curtains from the shrine and kneels before it. Barce hurries away and soon returns with a lighted candle, which she brings to her mistress. Dido lights the censer. Curtain.

ACT IV. SCENE 2

The same chamber in Dido's palace. The shrine of Sychæus is adorned with flowers; fire glows on the altar. Barce sits spinning at one side.

Dido is pacing the room with fierce energy. She goes to the window from time to time, then renews her fierce walking to and fro. Suddenly she presses her hand to her head as if a new thought had come to her. Her face assumes an expression of cunning. She picks up a golden goblet, and with a gesture to the old woman sends her to fill it.

When Barce has gone, Dido stealthily but quickly takes Æneas' sword from the wall, and, seating herself, with trembling fingers draws it from its scabbard. She feels the edge, shrinking in terror at the thought of her intended suicide. With a shudder, she presses the cold blade against her neck.

As she is thus meditating, her sister is heard coming. Dido quickly conceals the sword beneath the draperies of the couch. She assumes an air of gayety, kissing her sister and drawing her to a seat.

Dido (478-498):

I've found a way, my sister—give me joy—to bring

Him back to me, or free me from the love of him.

Hard by the confines of the Ocean in the west

The Æthiop country lies, where mighty Atlas holds

Upon his giant shoulders heaven's vault, all set

With stars. There dwells a priestess skilled in magic art,

Of the Massylian race, and guardian of the shrine

Of the Hesperides; her care, the dragon huge

To which she offers honeydew and soothing herbs,

The while she guards the precious boughs.—She claims the power

At will to free the soul from sorrow with her charms,

Or burden it with care; to stop the rapid stream,

And backward roll the stars; the shades of darkness too

Can she awake, and at her bidding shalt thou hear

The rumbling earth beneath thy feet, and see the trees

Descend the mountain slopes.—I swear it by the gods

And thee, unwillingly I seek the magic art.

Do thou within the palace rear a lofty pyre,

And place upon its top the faithless hero's arms

Which in his flight he left within our halls, yea all

That he has left, and then our wedding couch, my cause

Of woe, my heart is set to banish every trace

Of that perfidious one, and this the priestess bids.

Anna assents to her plan and hurries away to execute it. Dido quickly takes the sword from its hiding-place and in tremulous haste hangs it again upon the wall. Barce enters. Dido turns, fearing detection, but seeing that the old nurse has not suspected her, she takes the cup in her trembling fingers and drains it. Curtain.

ACT IV. SCENE 3

Dido's chamber, night. Dido is seated in the moonlight that streams through the open casement. A band of maidens, clad in white, are singing softly to her.

Chorus of maidens (apropos of 522-528):

[For music, see p. 81]

'T is eve; 't is night; a holy quiet broods

O'er the mute world—winds, waters are at peace;

The beasts lie couch'd amid unstirring woods,

The fishes slumber in the sounds and seas;

No twitt'ring bird sings farewell from the trees.

Hushed is the dragon's cry, the lion's roar;

Beneath her glooms a glad oblivion frees
The heart from care, its weary labors o'er,
Carrying divine repose and sweetness to its core.

[Selected from Tasso]

They quietly withdraw. Dido is convulsed with weeping.
Dido (529-532; 534-552):

But not for me, unhappy one, this night's sweet calm;
My cares redouble and o'erwhelm me with their flood.

She leaves the window and paces the room.

Ah me, what shall I do? My former suitors seek
And be again rejected? Shall I humbly court
Numidia's lords whose suit I have so often scorned?
Or shall I rather follow haughty Ilium's fleet,
Submissive to their every will?—Because in sooth,
'T is sweet to be delivered, and my former aid
Still dwells within their faithful memory? But who,
Though I should wish it, would permit me, or receive
The hated Dido in their haughty ships? Ah, poor,
Deluded one, dost thou not know, dost thou not still
Perceive the frailty of a Trojan oath? What then?
Shall I forsake my kingdom and accompany
The joyful sailors, or with all my Tyrian bands
Around me, follow in pursuit and force again
My friends upon the deep and bid them spread their sails,
My comrades whom with pain I weaned from Sidon's halls?
Nay, nay! as thou deservest, die, and with the sword
Thy sorrows end. O why was it not given me
To spend my life from wedlock and its sorrows free,

- 42 -

As beasts within their forest lairs? Or why, alas,

Was not my promise to Sychæus' ashes kept?

She sprinkles incense on the flame at the shrine of Sychæus. Dawn begins to brighten. The sailors are heard singing in the distance. Dido starts. She rushes to the window, and looking out, sees the Trojan fleet sailing away over the sea. She cries out in frenzy.

Dido (590-629):

Ye gods! and shall he go, and mock our royal power?

Why not to arms and send our forces in pursuit,

And bid them hurry down the vessels from the shore?

Ho there, my men, quick, fetch the torches, seize your arms,

And man the oars!—What am I saying? where am I?

What madness turns my brain? O most unhappy queen,

Is it thus thy evil deeds are coming back to thee?

Such fate was just when thou didst yield thy scepter up.—

Lo, there 's the fealty of him who, rumor says,

His country's gods with him in all his wandering bears

And on his shoulders bore his sire from burning Troy!

Why could I not have torn his body limb from limb,

And strewed his members on the deep? and slain his friends,

His son Ascanius, and served his mangled limbs

To grace his father's feast?—Such conflict might have had

A doubtful issue.—Grant it might, but whom had I,

Foredoomed to death, to fear? I might have fired his camp,

His ships, and wrapped in common ruin father, son,

And all the race, and given myself to crown the doom

Of all.—O Sun, who with thy shining rays dost see

All mortal deeds; O Juno, who dost know and thus

Canst judge the grievous cares of wedlock; thou whom wild

And shrieking women worship through the dusky streets,

O Hecate; and ye avenging Furies;—ye,

The gods of failing Dido, come and bend your power

To these my woes and hear my prayer. If yonder wretch

Must enter port and reach his land decreed by fate,

If thus the laws of Jove ordain, this order holds:

But, torn in war, a hardy people's foeman, far

From friends and young Iulus' arms, may he be forced

To seek a Grecian stranger's aid, and may he see

The death of many whom he loves. And when at last

A meager peace on doubtful terms he has secured,

May he no pleasure find in kingdom or in life;

But may he fall untimely, and unburied lie

Upon some solitary strand. This, this I pray,

And with my latest breath this final wish proclaim.

Then, O my Tyrians, with a bitter hate pursue

The whole accursèd race, and send this to my shade

As welcome tribute. Let there be no amity

Between our peoples. Rise thou from my bones,

O some avenger, who with deadly sword and brand

Shall scathe the Trojan exiles, now, in time to come,

Whenever chance and strength shall favor. Be our shores

To shores opposed, our waves to waves, and arms to arms,

Eternal, deadly foes through all posterity.

The servants rush in terrified during her passionate speech, and as she utters her curse, stand cowering before her. She dismisses with a gesture all except old Barce, who approaches her mistress.

(634-640):

Go, bring my sister Anna hither, dearest nurse:

In flowing water bid her haste to bathe her limbs,

And bring the rightful sacrifices of the flock.

So let her come. And thou with pious fillets gird

Thy temples; for to Stygian Jove my mind is fixed

To carry on the magic sacrifice begun,

And end my cares, and to devouring flames consign

The relics of that cursed son of Dardanus.

Barce totters away to do her bidding. Dido takes Æneas' mantle and sword from the wall, and unsheathes the sword.

(651-662):

Sweet pledges of my lord, while fate and god allowed,

Accept this soul of mine, and free me from my cares.

For I have lived and run the course that Fortune set;

And now my stately soul to Hades shall descend.

A noble city have I built; my husband's death

Have I avenged, and on my brother's head my wrath

Inflicted. Happy, ah too happy, had the keels

Of Troy ne'er touched my shores!—And shall I perish thus?—

But let me perish. Thus, oh thus, 't is sweet to seek

The land of shadows.—May the heartless Trojan see,

As on he fares across the deep, my blazing pyre,

And bear with him the gloomy omens of my death.

She rushes forth from the chamber in her frenzy. The sailors' chorus is repeated fainter and fainter. In a moment her death cry is heard. The servants rush in, and finding their mistress gone, hasten in the direction of her cry. Their lamentation is heard. They return bearing the body of the queen upon a couch. She has fainted, and upon her bosom the wound shows red and terrible. Anna enters, beside herself with grief.

Anna, kneeling beside the couch, addresses Dido, who revives enough to smile upon her sister (676-685):

Was it for this, O sister, thou didst seek to hide

Thy heart from me? Was this the meaning of the pyre,
And this the altar fires? What plaint in my despair
Shall I offer first? And didst thou spurn me, in thy death?
Thou shouldst instead have bidden me to share thy fate;
The selfsame moment should have reft the lives of both.
And with these impious hands did I thine altar rear,
And with this voice unto our country's gods appeal,
That, heartless, I might fail thee in this final hour?
O sister, here hast thou destroyed thyself and me,
Thy people, thy Sidonian fathers and thy realm.
With soothing water let me bathe her flowing wounds,
And if there hovers on her lips the fleeting breath,
With my own lips I claim it in the kiss of death.

The sailors' chorus sounds in the distance. Aroused by this, the dying queen half raises herself upon the couch. The servants throw open the casement and the Trojan ships are seen far away, sailing off over the sea.

Dido falls back lifeless. Curtain.

MUSIC
SONGS

PRELUDE

To be sung in unison before the curtain.

Ar - ma vi - rum - que ca - no, Tro - iae qui pri - mus ab o - ris

I - ta - li - am, fa - to pro - fu - gus, La - vi - na - que ve - nit

Li - to - ra, mul - tum il - le et ter - ris iac - ta - tus et al - to

Vi su - pe - rum, sae - vae me-mo - rem Iu - no - nis ob i - ram,
Mul - ta quo-qu° et bel - lo pas - sus, dum con - de - ret ur - bem,
In - fer - ret - que de - os La - ti - o: ge-nus un - de La - ti - num
Al - ba - ni - que pa - tres at - qu° al-tae moe - ni - a
Ro - mae. Mu - sa, mi - hi cau - sas me-mo - ra, quo
nu - mi - ne lae - so, Quid - ve do - lens, re - gi - na de -

um tot vol - ve-re ca - sus In - sig - nem pi - e -
ta - te vi-rum, tot ad - i - re la-bo - res Im - pu - le -
rit. Tan - tae - ne a - ni-mis cae - le - sti - bus i - rae?

HYMN TO THE DAWN

A CT I. S CENE 1

Chorus of Carthaginian Maidens

ro - ra!

Come,...... ro-sy-fin-gered god-dess of the dawn,

The saf - - fron couch of old Ti -

tho - - nus scorn - ing; Fling wide the gold - - en

port-als of the morn-ing, And bid the gloom-y mists of night be-

gone   Hail, Au - ro - ra, hail!

p
The
8va
p
dew - y stars have sped their si - lent flight, The
rit. cres. mf a tempo.
full - er glo - ries of thy rays ex - pect - ing; With
8va
8va
ro - sy beau - ty from a - far re - flect - ing, Thy
animando e crescendo
O - - - rient steeds come
animando e crescendo
pant - ing in - to sight.

- 53 -

ban - - - ners of thy gold - en light unfurled, The
a tempo e crescendo
crescendo
ban-ners of thy gold - - en light................. un -
ff
furled.
8va.........
8va.......

INVOCATION

ACT I. SCENE 3

dain That this may be a day of joy to us of
crescendo et accelerando
Tyre And these the Tro - jan ex - iles; let its
f
rit.
fame go down To our de - scendants, to our de -
tempo.
f
cres.
scend - - ants. May the god of wine and joy, And
rit.
p
f a tempo
FINE.
fos - t'ring, Ju - no, grace and cel - e-brate the day.
dim e rit.
f
p
D.S.*
Oh

SONG OF IOPAS

ACT I. SCENE 3

Adapted from Chopin, Nocturne in G minor

1. Of the orb of the wan-der-ing
4. Of the man-i-fold won-ders of

- 58 -

1st time.
shad - ows ap - pall, Till the men - ac - ing dark - ness flies;
god of the whole, Since the [omit.......................................]
2nd time.
Fine.
Solo
dawn of cre - a - tion be - gan.
2. Of the
all - po - tent for - ces that dwell in the air, With its
meas - ure - less reach - es of blue; The
soft float - ing clouds of...... gos - sa - mer there,

And the
loud - wail - ing storm - rack too;......... Of the
rain and the winds And the light - ning that blinds When its
swift - dart - ing bolt flash - es through;

Male Chorus, unaccompanied

3. Of the marvels deep hid in the bowels of earth, In the dark caves of Ocean confined, Where the rivers in slow trickling rills have their birth, And the dense tangled mazes unwind; In the deep underland, In the dim wonderland, Where broods the vast cosmical mind.

D. C.

SLUMBER SONG

ACT IV. SCENE 3 Chorus of Maidens

Words from Tasso; Ger. Lib. II. 96

O'er the mute world—winds, wa - ters are at peace.
The beasts lie couched amid un -
stir - ring woods, The fish - es slum-ber in the sounds and

seas; No twitt'ring bird sings farewell from the

trees. Hushed is the drag-on's cry,

the li-on's roar;

Be-neath her glooms a glad ob-liv-ion frees

The heart from care, its wea - ry la - bors o'er,
Car - ry - ing...... di - vine re - pose, Car - ry -
ing di - vine re - pose and sweetness to its
core,

Sweet-ness to its core, Sweet-ness to its

core.

II
The Fall of Troy

Illustrious Troy! renown'd in every clime

Through the long records of succeeding time;

Who saw protecting gods from heaven descend

Full oft, thy royal bulwarks to defend.

Though chiefs unnumber'd in her cause were slain,

With fate the gods and heroes fought in vain;

That refuge of perfidious Helen's shame

At midnight was involved in Grecian flame;

And now, by time's deep ploughshare harrow'd o'er,

The seat of sacred Troy is found no more.

No trace of her proud fabrics now remains,

But corn and vines enrich her cultured plains.

FALCONER, Shipwreck.

THE PERSONS OF THE DRAMA

ÆNEAS, son of Anchises and Venus, son-in-law of Priam, and, since the death of Hector, the leader of the Trojan war-chiefs.

PRIAM, king of Troy, now enfeebled by age.

ANCHISES, the aged father of Æneas.

LAOCOÖN, a son of Priam and priest of Apollo.

PANTHUS, a Trojan noble, priest of Apollo.

CORŒBUS, a Phrygian noble, ally of Priam, in love with Cassandra.

THE GHOST OF HECTOR.

ASCANIUS, son of Æneas and Creüsa (silent).

VENUS, the goddess of love, mother of Æneas.

HECUBA, wife of Priam.

CREÜSA, wife of Æneas.

CASSANDRA, daughter of Priam, reputed to be mad.

PYRRHUS, son of Achilles, leader of the Greeks in their final attack upon Troy.

SINON, a Greek tool, through whose treachery the Trojans were induced to admit the wooden horse within their walls.

ANDROGEOS, a Greek chieftain.

TROJAN warriors, nobles, and commons, shepherds, priestly attendants, boys, women, etc.

GREEK warriors.

ACT I

The Fall of Troy

ACT I. SCENE 1

The plain in front of Troy; the city walls; the sea; and, in the distance, Tenedos. Morning, without the gates. Joyful crowds of men, women, and children pour through the open doors. They gather about the strange wooden horse which stands without, and excitedly inquire what it means, and what shall be done with it. Thymoetes voices the sentiment of one party that it should be taken within the walls and set upon the citadel; while Capys and his adherents urge that they should examine the mystery where it stands, and destroy it. Great confusion reigns. The sentiment of Thymoetes seems about to prevail (26-39).

Enter Laocoön, running, followed by a band of priestly attendants, and shouting while still at some distance.

Laocoön (42-49):

What madness, wretched citizens, is this?

Can you believe your enemies have fled,

Or can you think that any gifts of Greeks

Are innocent of guile? So have you learned

To judge Ulysses? No, within this horse

The crafty Greeks are lying even now,

Or else its towering bulk has been contrived

To give them spying place upon our homes,

Or chance to scale our city's battlements.

Be sure some dark design is hidden here.

Trust not the horse, my friends; whate'er it is,

I fear the Greeks, though armed with gifts alone.

He hurls his spear, which sticks fast in the wooden horse and stands quivering there.

Scene 2

Enter Trojan shepherds, dragging in a man bound with thongs. They approach the king. The bystanders jibe at and mock the captive. The unknown stands as if bewildered and distraught, and at last cries (69-72):

Where now, alas, can I a refuge find

On land or sea? What chance of life remains

For one who can no longer claim a place

Among the Greeks? and now his bloody death

The vengeful sons of Dardanus demand.

The Trojans in wonder and with growing pity urge him to explain himself. He at last proceeds, having with an apparent effort regained his self control (77-104):

All things and truly will I tell to thee,

O king, whatever comes, nor will I seek

To hide that I am Grecian born. This first;

For though in woe my fate has plunged me deep
It shall not make me false and faithless too.
If any chance report has touched your ears
With Palamedes' name, great Belus' son,
Whom, though he was all innocent of guile,
Yet still, because his voice was ever raised
Against the war, by accusations false
The Greeks condemned, and sent to gloomy death;
But whom they now with fruitless grief lament:
To him my sire, while yet the war was young,
By poverty impelled, consigned his son
To serve the prince, by double ties endeared
Of blood and comradeship
While he in power
And in the councils of the kings stood high,
I, too, by his reflected light, enjoyed
Both name and fair renown. But when at last,
Through false Ulysses' murderous hate and guile,
(I speak what you do know), his death was wrought;
In deep distress, in darkness and in woe
I spent my days, and mourned the hapless fate
Of my poor friend. And, maddened by my grief,
I would not hold my peace, but loudly swore,
That if the fates of war should bring me back
As victor to my native land of Greece,
I should full vengeance take; and by my words
Dire hatred 'gainst my luckless self I roused.
Here was the fountain source of all my woes;
From now Ulysses, crafty enemy,

Began to spread vague hints among the Greeks,

Prefer strange charges, and to seek some cause

Against me, conscious in his heart of guilt.

Nor did he rest, until by Calchas' aid—

But why do I rehearse this senseless tale

To heedless ears? Or wherefore should I seek

To stay your hands, if 'tis enough to hear

That I am Greek, and in your hostile minds

All Greeks are judged alike.

Come, glut your hate

Upon me. For Ulysses would rejoice

To know that I am dead, and Atreus' sons

Would gladly purchase this with great reward.

Here the stranger pauses in seeming despair and resignation to his fate. The Trojans urge him to go on with his story. He resumes (108-144):

Full oft the Greeks, in utter weariness

Of that long siege, desired to abandon Troy,

And seek their homes again. Oh, that they had!

But whensoe'er they addressed them to the sea,

Rough wintry blasts and storms affrighted them.

And when this horse, of wooden timbers framed,

Completed stood, a votive offering,

The winds from every quarter of the heavens

Howled threateningly. To seek the will of Heaven,

The anxious Greeks despatch Eurypylus

To Phœbus' oracle. He straight reports

Apollo's mandate grim and terrible:

"Before, O Greeks, ye sailed to Troia's shores,

Ye first had need to appease the angry winds

With bloody sacrifice—a maiden's death
E'en so, by blood must your return be sought;
Again must Grecian life atonement make."
When this dire oracle among the crowd,
From ear to ear, from lip to lip was spread,
They stood with horror stunned, and chilling fear
Their inmost hearts with dire forebodings filled.
They trembling ask for whom the fates prepare,
Whom does Apollo seek in punishment?
Then comes the Ithacan with clamor loud,
The prophet Calchas dragging in our midst,
And bids with charge insistent that he tell
The will of heaven. And now from many lips
The grim forebodings of Ulysses' guile
Assail my ears, while all in silence wait
To see the end. Ten days the seer was mute,
Hid in his tent, refusing steadily
By word of his to doom a man to death.
At length, his feigned reluctance at an end,
And goaded by Ulysses' clamors loud,
He spoke, and named me as the sacrifice.
All gave assent; and while each feared a doom
Which might befall himself, they calmly bore
When on my wretched head they saw it light.
And now the day of horror was at hand.
All things were ready for the sacrifice;
The salted meal was sprinkled on my head,
And round my brows the fatal fillets twined.
Then, I confess it, did I break my bonds.

I fled from death and in the sedgy reeds

Along the muddy margin of a lake

All night I lay in hiding, hoping there

To lurk until their homeward sails were spread.

And now my country dear I ne'er shall see,

My darling children and my aged sire

Whose face I long to see. But they are doomed

To pay the penalty which I escaped,

And by their death repair this fault of mine.

But by the gods above, divinities

Who with impartial eyes behold the truth,

If anywhere there still abides with men

Unsullied faith, I beg you, pity me

Who have endured so dire a weight of woe,

A soul that has been foully overborne.

The Trojans are moved to tears by this tale of woe; and Priam bids the chains be stricken from him. He then addresses the prisoner with friendly words.

Priam (148-151):

Whoe'er thou art, away with thoughts of Greeks.

Be man of ours. And, as I question thee,

Give true reply. What means this monster horse?

Who first proposed, and what its purpose here?

Is it some votive gift, or does it stand

Against our walls as enginery of war?

Sinon stretches his freed hands to the heavens. He speaks excitedly and as one inspired.

Sinon (154-194):

O ye eternal fires, be witness now,

Ye heavenly stars, divine, inviolate,

Ye cursed knives, and altars which I fled,

Ye fillets which as victim doomed I wore:

'Tis right for me to break all sacred oaths

Which bound me to the Greeks; 'tis right to hate,

And blab their secrets to the common air.

I'll not be held by any ties of land

Or law. Do thou but keep thy promises,

O Troy, and, saved by me, keep plighted faith,

If I with truth shall make thee rich returns.

Recovering himself, he goes on more quietly, and with an air of perfect sincerity.

The Greeks' whole hope and confidence in war

Had rested from the first on Pallas' aid.

But from the time when godless Diomede,

And that curst Ithacan, expert in crime,

Dared desecrate the goddess' sacred fane,

Dared drag her mystic image forth, and kill

Her faithful guard, and on her virgin locks

Lay bloody, lustful hands unconsecrate:

From then their hopes kept ebbing back and back,

Their powers were shattered and their goddess' aid

Denied. And she with no uncertain signs

Revealed at once her outraged deity.

Scarce had the sacred image reached the camp,

When glittering flames blazed from the staring eyes,

And salty perspiration down her limbs

Went streaming; and, oh wonderful to say,

Thrice from the ground, accoutered as she was

With shield and quivering spear, the image leaped.

Straitway did Calchas prophecy that all
Must forth again in flight upon the sea;
That Troy could never by Argolic arms
Be overthrown, save as they back again
To sacred Argos fared and there regained
That heavenly favor which they first had brought
To Ilium.
And now have they indeed
Gone back to Greece, to seek fresh auspices,
And win once more the blessing of the gods.
And soon, and suddenly, the sea retraced,
Will they be here again. So Calchas bade.
Meanwhile, by that same prophet warned, did they
This wooden image fashion to appease
Th' offended goddess, and atonement make
To her outraged divinity. And more—
The prophet bade them form an image huge
Of oaken beams, of such proportions vast
That through no gate of Troy could it be led,
Nor set within the walls, lest thus once more
The people from their ancient deity
Protection find. For if Minerva's gift
Should by your hands be desecrated, then
Would dreadful doom (Heaven send it on their heads)
Upon old Priam and his Phrygians come;
But if within your walls this sacred horse
Should by your voluntary hands be set,
Then would all Asia rise with one accord,
And sweep in mighty war against the Greeks,

And that dire doom upon our grandsons fall.

SCENE 3

The Trojans are entirely satisfied with this explanation and treat Sinon with respectful consideration. At this juncture, two huge serpents come up out of the sea, and, while the people flee shrieking away on all sides, they make their way to Laocoön where he stands sacrificing at the altar, and enfold him and his two sons in their deadly coils (195-227).

SCENE 4

Great excitement follows. People say that Laocoön has perished justly, since he impiously violated the sacred horse, and loudly demand that the creature be taken within the walls (228-249):

A voice from the crowd:

Oh, dreadful punishment, but well deserved,

For with his impious spear he smote the oak,

The sacred wood to Pallas consecrate.

Another voice:

Now haste we and within our city lead

This horse portentous, and with humble prayer

Minerva's aid and pardoning favor seek.

They hastily enlarge the gate, attach ropes to the horse, and put rollers under its feet, many willing hands lay hold of the ropes and pull the horse along. Boys and girls dance and sing around the workers. The horse sticks at the threshold of the gate, and Cassandra, who has been looking on as one entranced, cries out forebodingly.

Cassandra:

O fatherland! O Ilium, home of gods!

Ye walls of Troy, in war illustrious!

See there, upon the threshold of the gate,

The monster halts—again—and yet again!

And from its rumbling hold I hear the sound

Of clashing arms! O Troy! O fatherland!

But the people, not heeding her, press on and disappear within the city walls with the wooden horse, on the way to the citadel. Everywhere are heard sounds of delirious joy.

ACT II

ACT II. SCENE 1

Night. The chamber of Æneas. He lies sleeping calmly upon his couch. Enter Ghost of Hector, wan and terrible, bearing in his hands the sacred images of the Penates.

Æneas, starting up to a sitting posture, as if talking in a dream (281-286):

O light of Troy, O prop of Trojan hopes,

What slow delays have held thee from our sight,

O long awaited one? Whence com'st thou here?

We see thee now, with hardships overborne,

But only after many of thy friends

Have met their doom, and after struggles vast

Of city and of men.—But what, alas,

Has so defiled thy features? Whence these wounds

And horrid scars I see?

Hector, with deep sighs and groans (289-295):

Oh, get thee hence,

Thou son of Venus, flee these deadly flames.

Our foemen hold the walls; our ancient Troy

Is fallen from her lofty pinnacle

Enough for king and country has been done;

If Troy could have been saved by any hand,

This hand of mine would have defended her.

But now to thee she trusts her sacred gods

And all their sacred rites; take these with thee

As comrades of thy fates; seek walls for these,

Which, when the mighty deep thou hast o'ercome,

Thou shalt at length in lasting empire set.

He makes as if to give the sacred images to Æneas, and vanishes.

A confused sound of distant shouting and clashing of arms fills the room. Æneas leaps from his couch, now fully awake, and stands with strained and attentive ears. The truth dawns upon him as the sounds grow clearer, and as he can see from his window the red flames of burning Troy. He snatches up his arms and is rushing from the room when Panthus hurries in bearing sacred images in his hands and leading his little grandson.

Æneas (322):

My friend, where lies the battle's central point?

What stronghold do we keep against the foe?

Panthus (324-335):

The last, the fated day of Troy is come.

The mighty glory of the Trojan state

Is of the past, and we, alas, no more

May call ourselves of Ilium; for lo,

The cruel gods have given all to Greece,

And foemen lord it in our blazing town;

The great horse stands upon our citadel,

And from his roomy side pours armed men;

While Sinon, gloating o'er his victory,

With blazing torch is busy everywhere.

Down at the double gates still others press

For entrance, all Mycenæ's clamorous hosts,

And weapons thick beset the narrow streets.

In battle order stand the long drawn lines

Of gleaming steel prepared for deadly strife.

Scarce do the sturdy watchmen of the gates

Attempt to hold their posts against the foe,

But in the smothering press fight blindly on.

At this, Æneas joins Panthus and together they rush out into the city.

SCENE 2

A street of Troy, lit by the moonlight and the glare of burning buildings. Trojans rush in from different sides and rally to Æneas.

Æneas (348-354):

O comrades, O ye hearts most brave in vain,

If you have steadfast minds to follow one

On desperate deeds intent, you see our case:

The gods, who long have buttressed up our state,

Have fled their sacred altars and their shrines,

And left us to our fate. You seek to aid

A city wrapped in flames. Then let us die

And in the midst of death our safety find:

Our safety's single hope—to hope for none.

The little band hurries off toward the noise of battle in neighboring streets. Enter from the other direction straggling bands of Greeks, drunk with victory. They burn and pillage on all sides, temples and homes alike. Re-enter Trojans led by Æneas. Androgeos, a Greek, thinking them to be Greeks, goes up to them.

Androgeos (373-375):

Now haste ye, men; what time for sloth is this?

The rest on fire and pillage are intent,

While you but now address you to the task.

Androgeos suddenly perceives that these are foes, and is struck dumb with amazement. The Trojans rush upon him and slay him together with the others of his band.

Corœbus, one of Æneas' band, exultingly (387-391):

O friends, where kindly fortune first doth show

The path of safety, let us follow there.

With these slain Greeks let us our shields exchange,

Their helms and breastplates let us don, and so

In all things seem as Greeks. When foemen strive,

Who questions aught of trickery or might?

Our foes against themselves shall lend us arms.

They exchange arms with the dead Greeks. Thus arrayed, they mingle with the parties of Greeks who straggle in, and slay them. The Greeks, not understanding this strange turn of affairs, flee away in terror. This action is repeated at intervals several times.

Enter a band of Greeks led by Ajax, the Atridæ, and others, dragging Cassandra roughly along by the hair. Her hands are tied with thongs. Corœbus, though the odds are overwhelmingly against him, rushes in to save his beloved Cassandra. The other Trojans, because of their disguise of Greek armor, are attacked by their own friends stationed at near by points of vantage, and now the Greeks themselves, recognizing the ruse at last, overwhelm the little Trojan band by force of numbers. Other Greeks pour in from all sides and add their testimony that these are Trojans. In the desperate encounter many of the Trojans fall.

Æneas performs Herculean feats of arms, and slays many Greeks, but is himself unhurt. At last he and a few followers escape into a street leading to Priam's palace, whence loud and continued shouting can be heard.

Scene 3

At Priam's palace (viewed from without), desperately attacked by Greeks and defended by Trojans. (a) The assailants attempt by scaling ladders to mount to the flat, turreted roof of the palace, while the defendants hurl down upon these darts and stones, and pry off whole towers which fall with a mighty crash. The air is filled with the thunderous noise of these falling masses and with the other confused shouts and sounds of a desperate conflict.

(b) Pyrrhus with a strong band of Greeks is endeavoring to batter down the gates of the palace at its main entrance.

SCENE 4

Priam's palace from within. All is confusion and terror. Women rush from room to room, with disheveled hair streaming, and with cries of wild despair. A crowded mass of men are attempting to defend the main entrance. Overhead can be seen and heard the defenders on the roof opposing the attack from without.

In the central open court of the palace, upon the steps of a great altar overshadowed by a laurel tree, Hecuba and a group of women have seated themselves, huddling there in the hope of protection from the sanctity of the altar. Suddenly old Priam comes out into the court, hurriedly adjusting his armor.

Hecuba, calling to him (519-524):

What dost thou there, of reason all bereft,

O wretched husband? What avail those arms?

Or whither speedest thou with tottering steps?

Such aid and such defense as thou canst give

Cannot avail us now, nor Hector's self,

Could he come back to us. Come hither then;

These sacred altar stairs shall shield us all,

Or in their sight will we together die.

Priam joins the women at the altar.

But see, Polites comes, by Pyrrhus pressed;

Through hostile arms, through halls and colonnades,

He flees alone in sore distress of wounds,

While Pyrrhus follows hard with deadly aim.

And now, Oh, now he grasps and thrusts him through.

Polites falls dead at the feet of Priam and Hecuba.

Priam, springing up and facing Pyrrhus (535-543):

For that base crime of thine, that impious deed,

I pray the gods, if there are gods in heaven

Who care for men, to grant thee dire return,

And give thee what thou hast so richly earned.

For thou hast slain my son before my face,

And with his blood defiled his father's eyes.

But that Achilles, whom thou falsely claim'st

As sire, did not so treat his royal foe,

But held in reverence the sacred laws.

My Hector's corpse he gave for burial

And sent me back in safety to my home.

He hurls his spear with feeble strength at Pyrrhus. The spear sticks ineffectually in the opposing shield.

Pyrrhus, scornfully (547-550):

Then bear this message to my noble sire:

Fail not to tell him all my impious deeds,

And how unworthy has his Pyrrhus proved.

Now die.

He drags the old man to the altar and slays him there. Exit Pyrrhus, leaving the bloody corpse of the old man upon the ground. The women are carried off as prisoners by the Greeks who now come thronging in.

Scene 5

In the now deserted palace near the shrine of Vesta. Helen is lurking for protection within the shrine.

Æneas, passing by and seeing Helen (577-587):

Shall this, the common scourge of friend and foe,

Unscathed, behold her native land again?

Her husband, home, her sire and children see?

Shall she as conquering queen go proudly back,

Attended by a throng of Trojan slaves?

Shall Troy have burned for this, old Priam die,
And all the Trojan plain have reeked with blood?
It shall not be. No fame, I know, is earned
By woman's punishment; such victory
Has little praise; but yet I shall be praised
For having utterly destroyed this wretch,
And on her head inflicted vengeance dire.
It will be sweet to feed my passion's flame,
And satisfy the ashes of my friends.

He is rushing into the shrine with drawn sword when suddenly Venus appears before him.

Venus (594-620):

What grief inflames thee to this boundless wrath?
What madness this, my son? And whither, pray,
Has fled thy care for us? Bethink thee, first,
Where thou hast left thy father, spent with age;
Whether thy wife, Creüsa, still survives;
Bethink thee of Ascanius thy son.
For they are hemmed about on every side
By hostile Greeks; but for my shielding care,
Already would the flames have swept them off,
And swords of enemies have drunk their blood.
'Tis not the beauty of the Spartan queen
That should arouse thy hate, nor shouldst thou blame
Thy kinsman, Paris; for the cruel gods,
The gods, I say, have laid thy city low,
And overthrown the lofty walls of Troy.
Behold—for I will straight remove the mist
Which, dense and clinging, clouds thy mortal sight;

Do thou but be obedient to my words;—

Here, where thou seest huge masses overthrown,

Rocks torn from rocks, commingled smoke and dust,

Great Neptune with his trident's fearful stroke

Causes the walls to rock upon their base.

Here Juno, first of all, with savage mien,

Besets the Scæan gates, and, girt with steel,

In fury calls her allies from the ships.

Now turn thine eyes unto the citadel,

And there behold Tritonian Pallas stand,

All blazing with the war-cloud's lurid glare,

And that fell Gorgon's head. Nay Jove himself

Inspires the Greeks with courage, gives them strength,

And whets the gods against the Trojans' arms.

Betake thee then to flight and end thy toils.

For I will never leave thee, till at last

I bring thee safely to thy father's house.

Æneas, overcome by these revelations, and resigned to fate, retires.

ACT III

ACT III. SCENE 1

The atrium in the palace of Æneas. The aged Anchises lies prone upon the couch. Creüsa, Ascanius, and other members of the household are huddled together in the same room, listening in awestruck silence to the confused sounds of battle without. The room is lit by the red glare of burning buildings. Enter Æneas, breathless with his haste.

Æneas, going up to his father and attempting to lift him in his arms (635, 636):

O father, all is lost; come, flee with me,

While still the fates and angry gods allow;
Come, let me bear thee on my shoulders broad
Unto the shelter of Mount Ida's slopes.

Anchises, resisting (637-649):

If all is o'er, and Troy is in the dust,
Why should I wish to prolong this worthless life
In exiled wanderings? Turn ye to flight,
Who feel the blood of youth within your veins,
Whose sturdy powers still flourish in their prime.
If heavenly gods had wished me still to live,
They would have saved this home wherein to dwell.
Enough and more, that I have seen one fall
Of Troy, and once outlived my captured town.
Then, even as I lie in seeming death,
Address my lifeless body and be gone.
I'll quickly gain the boon of death I seek:
The enemy will pity me and slay,
Or else will slay me for my noble spoils.
As for the loss of burial due the dead,
'Twill not be hard to bear. Too long on earth
I spend my useless years, abhorred of heaven,
Since when the sire of gods and king of men
Blasted my body with his lightning's breath,
And marked me with his scorching bolt of flame.

Æneas and all the household join in entreating Anchises to go with them (651-653):

The heavy hand of fate is on us all,
But do not thou, O father, seek to add

To this our weight of sorrow, and o'erthrow
Our fortunes utterly.

But the old man stubbornly persists in his refusal.
Æneas, seeing his father immovable (656-670):

And didst thou think that I could leave thee here,
O father, and betake myself to flight?
And has such monstrous utterance as this
Fall'n from a father's lips? If heaven has willed
That nothing from this city vast survive,
And if thy mind is firmly set to die,
And 'tis thy pleasure to our ruined Troy
To add thyself and all thy family—
The door to that destruction opens wide
Soon Pyrrhus will be here, his murderous hands
Reeking with Priam's blood, who slays the son
Before his father's eyes, and eke the sire
Upon the sacred altar's very steps
Was it for this that thou, through sword and flame,
O fostering mother, didst deliver me,
That midst the very sanctities of home
I should behold the foe, that I should see
Ascanius, my father, and my wife
All weltering in one another's blood?
Nay rather, arms! My men, in haste bring arms!

Attendants bring him his sword and shield which he hurriedly fits in place.

The last day calls the vanquished to their death.
Let me go forth to meet the Greeks again,
Once more sustain the desperate battle shock.

We shall not all in helpless slaughter die.

Æneas is rushing toward the door, when Creüsa intercepts him, pushing toward him their little son, Ascanius.

Creüsa, kneeling (675-678):

If thou art going forth to seek thy death,

Oh, take us, too, with thee to share thy fate;

But if thy wisdom bids thee still to hope

In sword and shield, here make thy final stand,

And guard thy home. To whose protection, pray,

Is young Iulus left, to whose thy sire?

To whom can I, once called thy wife, appeal?

Suddenly a tongue of flame is seen to leap and play among the locks of the boy. His parents, in consternation, attempt to extinguish this, but to no effect.

Anchises, seeing the portent, starts up with wondering joy, stretching his hands upward in prayer (689-691):

O Jove, if thou art moved by any prayer,

Look on us now; this only do I ask;

And, if our piety deserves the boon,

Help us, O father, and confirm these signs.

A sudden crash of thunder resounds without, and through the open impluvium a bright star is seen shooting across the sky.

Anchises, rising from his couch in trembling haste (701-704):

Now, now is no delay; I'll follow thee,

O son, wherever thou wouldst have me go.

O gods, on whom our fatherland depends,

Preserve my house, preserve my grandson too.

From you has come this heavenly augury,

And on your will divine does Ilium rest.

I yield me then, O son, into thy hands.

And would no more refuse to go with thee.

Meanwhile from without the glare of the conflagration increases, and the shouting of the victorious Greeks is heard approaching nearer and nearer.

Æneas (707-720):

Come then, dear father, mount upon my back,

For on my shoulders will I carry thee,

Nor will I find that burden overhard.

Whatever comes, 'twill come to both of us,

We'll share misfortune and deliverance too.

He takes the old man upon his shoulders, first spreading over his back a lion's skin.

Let young Iulus fare along with me,

But at a distance let my wife note well

The way I take. And ye, attendants, hark

To what I say. Without the city walls

There is a mound, where stands an ancient fane

Of Ceres, all alone, a cypress tree

Of ancient stock, preserved with reverent care

For many generations, overhangs

The temple walls. Be this our meeting place

To which by devious ways in many bands

We all shall come.

Do thou, my father, carry in thy hands

The sacred emblems and our household gods;

For me, late come from strife, and stained with blood,

'Twere sacrilege to touch the holy things,

Till I have cleansed me in some running stream.

With his father upon his shoulders and leading Iulus by the hand he takes his way out of the house. The household follows, leaving the room deserted.

Scene 2

A dark street near the Ida gate. Æneas, Anchises, and Ascanius as before. Suddenly through the darkness there comes the distant sound of feet and shouting as of pursuers.

Anchises, peering in the direction of the sound (733, 734):

Oh, speed thy steps, my son; the foe are near;

I see their gleaming shields and flashing spears.

At this Æneas hastens his steps and leaves the scene, his band hurrying after him.

Scene 3

At the ancient temple of Ceres without the walls. The fugitives come straggling in in various bands, a motley array, Æneas and his immediate followers among the rest. Æneas watches them as they come and gather about him, counting and identifying them. He now discovers that Creüsa is missing.

Æneas (738-748):

Alas, Creüsa, by what wretched fate

Hast thou been overwhelmed? Where art thou now?

Hast wandered from the way, or, spent with toil,

Hast thou given o'er the journey? Woe is me!

My eyes shall never more behold thy face!

What god or man is guilty of this crime?

Or what more cruel deed have I beheld

In all our stricken town?

To his friends:

Behold, my friends,

To you my son and sire and household gods

Do I commend, while I reseek the streets

And ruined dwellings of our fallen Troy,

If haply I may find her once again.

He puts on his full armor, and rushes back through the dark gate into the city.

Scene 4

A deserted street in Troy, lit up fitfully by smoldering fires. Æneas enters, peering through the gloom on all sides, and calling loudly upon the name of his wife. Suddenly a shadowy form appears before him.

The Ghost of Creüsa (776-789):

What boots it to indulge this storm of grief,

O dearest husband? For be sure of this,

That not without permission of the gods

Have these things come to pass. 'Twas not allowed

That thy Creüsa should go hence with thee,

Nor does Olympus' ruler suffer it.

To distant lands, long exiled must thou roam,

Must plow the water of the vasty deep,

Until thou come to that far western land,

Where Lydian Tiber's gently murmuring stream

Rolls down through rich and cultivated fields.

There joyful state and kingdom wait for thee,

There one who is allotted for thy wife.

Then dry the tears which now affection sheds

For thy well-loved Creüsa, once thy wife;

For 'tis not mine to see the haughty seats

Of Myrmidonian or Dolopian foes;

Nor shall I go to serve the Grecian dames,

Proud princess of Dardania that I am,

By marriage made the child of Venus' self.

But Cybele, great mother of the gods,

Detains me still upon these Trojan shores.

Then look thy last upon me, and farewell,

And let our common son employ your love.

Æneas starts forward with a cry to embrace the ghost, but it eludes his grasp and vanishes from sight. He sorrowfully turns away and leaves the scene.

SCENE 5

The gray dawn breaks; Mount Ida looms dimly in the distance; the exiles a weary, discouraged band of men, women, and children, take their way out into the unknown world.

Milton Keynes UK
Ingram Content Group UK Ltd.
UKHW030851011224
451361UK00001B/102

9 789362 514844